TREASURES FROM THE SANCTUARY

FOR THE

———————— ❧ ————————

BODY

TREASURES FROM THE SANCTUARY

FOR THE

BODY

Tanya Wheway

with Jane Ross-Macdonald

Thorsons
An Imprint of HarperCollins*Publishers*

Thorsons
An Imprint of HarperCollins*Publishers*
77–85 Fulham Palace Road
Hammersmith, London W6 8JB

Published by Thorsons 1998
1 3 5 7 9 10 8 6 4 2

© Tanya Wheway 1998

Tanya Wheway asserts the moral right to
be identified as the author of this work

A catalogue record for this book
is available from the British Library

ISBN 0 7225 3768 9

The quotes given in this series of books for the
Mind, Body and Spirit form part of a collection
Tanya Wheway has gathered over many years. For this
reason not all of them are attributed, but the publishers
are anxious to trace any copyright holders that have
not been contacted for permission.

The Sanctuary and the Single Fish Device are the trade mark
of The Sanctuary at Covent Garden Ltd

Text illustrations by Daisy Kelly

Printed and bound in Great Britain by
Woolnoughs Bookbinding Ltd, Irthlingborough, Northants

DEDICATION

I would like to dedicate this set of three books for the mind, body and spirit to my amazingly wonderful family who I love very dearly: husband, business partner and lover, Allan, son Mark and his wife Katherine, daughter Samantha, her husband Jon and grandchildren Emily-Anne and James, also my great parents, Micky and Norman. They have all really made my life totally complete and I would like to thank them for all their love, and also for their understanding and the support they have always given me in respect of all the hours I spend working.

I would like to thank the Sanctuary team, particularly Spa Managers Kirsty Skvan, Helen Smith and Sarah Morgans, The Sanctuary Fitness Club Manager Oonagh Yeo and Nutritonist Maria Davies for their assistance and support. A big thank you to Jane Ross-Macdonald for all that she has contributed to the book and for keeping me on track, Wanda Whitely for opening the doors and being such an inspiration and Nicola Vimpany for her tremendous patience and warm, experienced support.

PREFACE

The Sanctuary in Covent Garden, London, came of age in 1998 as it celebrated its 21st anniversary as a Day Spa exclusively for women. In celebration we have launched this series of *Treasures from the Sanctuary:* one for the *Mind,* one for the *Body* and one for the *Spirit.* We hope they will provide you with words of wisdom and wit to inform, amuse and inspire.

In 1964 an American dancer/choreographer, Gary Cockrell, opened our London premises as the famous Dance Centre, frequented by talented dancers and actors such as Nureyev, Gene Kelly, Dustin Hoffman and Sir John Gielgud. Today the tradition of exercising the body continues with The Sanctuary Fitness Club, exclusively for women.

The Sanctuary philosophy is a holistic one, encompassing mind, body and spirit, which nurtures all the senses. Paintings and candlelight delight the eye, essential oils fragrance the air, fresh produce titillates the taste buds, expert hands pamper the body and the sound of fountains and beautiful music soothe the mind and soul.

INTRODUCTION

'The body is a sacred garment. It's your first and last garment, it is what you enter life in and what you depart life with, and it should be treated with honour.'
Martha Graham

When we are young and when we have our health we take it for granted. We think of it as a birthright, rather than the precious gift it is. Sadly it is often only when we become threatened with a serious illness or possible loss of life that we are prepared to invest time, effort and money in taking care of our body. Likewise, for those of us who are fortunate to have a long life it may not be until we are in our fifties or sixties that we start to appreciate that our bodies would be in much better shape, with minimal discomfort, and would carry on serving us well if we became more knowledgeable and took better care of ourselves.

The great news is that even if you have abused or neglected your body for a number of years, it will still, quite quickly, respond positively to a new health and fitness regimen. However, I would stress that fewer years of abuse and more years of care will make a big difference.

We hope that this little book will inspire you to treat your body with the love and respect it deserves: the dividends can be priceless.

With warmest wishes to you from the Sanctuary team.

Tanya Wheway
Managing Director
The Sanctuary, Covent Garden

HOW TO USE THIS BOOK

We have endeavoured in this small book to give you practical information on how to take better care of your most important asset: without our health we have nothing.

Respecting that everyone's time is incredibly precious, and usually in short supply, we have created a style which is easy to dip into. The alphabetical listing will enable you to find material that is appropriate for you at any given moment.

Our approach at The Sanctuary is to seduce people into health, rather than beat them into it. Getting fit and healthy should and can be fun! The quotations given in our series of books for the mind, body and spirit have been collected over many years. I hope you find them useful, inspirational and amusing: remember that laughter is the best medicine!

The mind, body and spirit are inextricably linked. This little book focuses on your physical well-being, but some of the techniques in *Treasures for the Mind* should help you make these changes and achieve your goals.

ACUPUNCTURE AND ACUPRESSURE

The Chinese believe there are channels of energy running through the body, called meridians. When our body's energy, or Qi (pronounced 'chee'), is in balance we are healthy; when it is out of balance we become ill. By inserting fine needles into certain points on the body, the acupuncturist aims to restore this balance. In the case of acupressure, fingers and thumbs, rather than needles, place pressure on the acupuncture points of the body and thus help rebalance the Qi. While you need to consult a qualified practitioner for acupuncture, one of the wonderful things about acupressure is that it can be done anywhere. You do not have to be undressed or lying on a special table, and the only equipment you need is a friend and a pair of hands. Self-help books will guide you in how to use acupressure for specific problems, but for serious ailments a professional therapist is strongly recommended.

'An archaeologist is the best husband a woman can have; the older she gets, the more interested he is in her.'

Agatha Christie

'Every season of our lives holds a beauty all of its own.'

'Don't complain about getting old … some people never get the chance.'

'You don't stop playing because you grow old – you grow old because you stop playing.'

Mr Sloan Senior

'Isn't love the greatest refreshment in life?'

Picasso, aged 90

AGEING

Look at getting older not as the using up of resources but as the accumulation of riches. This book aims to give you inspiration to make the most of your body, to take care of yourself better and to enjoy your life to the full without allowing the ravages of time to take too great a toll. The mind plays a very important part, and attitude is key, but you can also slow down the effects of age by:

- exercise (*see p43*) and good posture
- stepping up your intake of the 'antioxidant' vitamins, A, C and E, plus selenium and beta carotene
- eating a moderate, balanced diet with limited junk food
- giving up smoking and too much caffeine
- a regular intake of pure water (avoid fizzy drinks)
- getting fresh air, a little sunshine and quality sleep
- limiting alcohol consumption to a healthy one or two units a day
- establishing a good rapport with your doctor and complementary therapists

- drinking St John's wort tea or kava kava tea to help with depression and emotional balance
- eating tofu, soya milk or soya yogurt to help stave off osteoporosis
- taking ginkgo biloba to help circulation and memory, and dong quai for balancing hormones and reducing hot flushes
- learning relaxation and meditation techniques and how to breathe effectively (*see p23*)
- learning not to 'think old': court the company of young people as well as contemporaries, seek new experiences and avoid ruts and routines.

ALCOHOL

Alcohol is a poison. It damages the liver, heart and mental faculties, robs the body of nutrients and can destroy your appearance. Popularly misconceived as a stimulant, alcohol is in fact a depressant: the initial lift is followed by a let-down. In moderation alcohol promotes relaxation and increases the levels of HDLs (high density lipo-proteins) which are the protective part of cholesterol.

Wine is the most acceptable form of alcohol: it can have a beneficial effect on the heart, its enzymes aid digestion and it can provide some B vitamins and minerals. Organic, chemical-free wine is best. Spirits, on the other hand, rob the body of vitamins and water. Remember too that alcohol is calorie-rich and if you are watching your weight it is preferable to eat, rather than drink, your calories.

ALEXANDER TECHNIQUE

The Alexander Technique, which cannot be taught effectively from a book but really needs the help of a teacher, is a remarkable system of gentle posture exercises developed by an Australian actor/reciter.

Alexander Technique can address neck, back and shoulder pain, breathing disorders, stress and general fatigue, where misuse and imperfect balance are contributing factors. It can help you to improve your co-ordination and performance as a sports player, or simply enhance your sense of well-being.

A course, which may be 12 sessions or more, can improve posture, movement, breathing, circulation and clarity of thought, and develop a new sense of balance within the mind and body.

ALLERGIES AND FOOD
INTOLERANCES

Most people know if they are allergic to nuts, tomatoes, or strawberries by their immediate and often violent reaction. However, many common chronic conditions can also be due to an intolerance or sensitivity to certain foods. Keep a food diary, noting what you eat and any adverse reactions you experience in order to pinpoint the culprits. Common causes are dairy products and wheat, but to be sure you could have your symptoms checked out by a kinesiologist or nutritionist. Symptoms of an allergy or intolerance can include: asthma, irritable bowel syndrome, eczema, hay fever, joint pains, migraine, constipation and diarrhoea.

ANTIBIOTICS

Antibiotics, when used correctly, save lives. However, they also kill off 'friendly' bacteria in the gut which play a vital role in keeping our bodies going. Over-use of antibiotics can lead to liver problems, bladder infections, arthritic conditions, premenstrual and menopausal symptoms and chronic bowel problems. Some experts believe that up to 70% of antibiotics are wrongly prescribed, which not only damages our body's internal ecology but also leads to the emergence of resistant strains of bacteria.

A healthy body will usually fight infections on its own. Protect your immune system by reducing the following immunity-suppressing elements: sugar, alcohol, caffeine, medical drugs, smoking, stress, over-exercise, lack of rest, excess weight and an insufficient intake of nutrients. Step up your intake of foods containing selenium, zinc, B vitamins, garlic and friendly bacteria such as acidophilus and bifidobacteria. Consider complementary therapies for balancing your body's energy. Herbalists can recommend a wide range of antibiotic alternatives.

AROMATHERAPY

For centuries the pure essences of aromatic plants have been valued for their luxurious fragrances and their many life-enhancing properties. This ancient healing art harnesses the unique therapeutic powers of essential oils together with relaxing and restorative massage techniques to treat common ailments as well as promote good health and emotional well-being.

Aromatherapy massage works mainly on the nervous system, helping to protect the immune system and energize or stabilize emotions. Penetration of the oils is through both inhalation and the skin.

Some popular oils include:

- bergamot for depression, anxiety and for promoting restful sleep
- chamomile for skin irritations and for helping with emotional unease
- clary sage for period pains and for release of muscular tension

- ⚬ eucalyptus for colds, flu and for reducing fevers and aches and pains
- ⚬ geranium for menopausal symptoms, oily skins and for balancing mood swings
- ⚬ jasmine for enhanced libido
- ⚬ lavender for sunburn and insect bites, and for calming the emotions
- ⚬ neroli for shock and depression
- ⚬ peppermint for an alert mind and for easing sore throats and congestion
- ⚬ rosemary for muscular aches, scalp problems and for enhancing mental clarity
- ⚬ tea tree for its antiseptic and antibacterial properties.

ASTHMA

The incidence of asthma is increasing, with 3 million sufferers in Britain alone, and up to one in three children suffering from wheezing.

The following measures can cut down on attacks, or reduce the possibility of developing asthma:

- ✿ Clean curtains, carpets and upholstery regularly.
- ✿ Open windows.
- ✿ Don't have the central heating up too high.
- ✿ Change pot pourri frequently, or avoid it altogether.
- ✿ Use a new style of vacuum cleaner that does not spit out dust.
- ✿ Buy special mattress and pillow covers.
- ✿ Avoid perfumes and room sprays.
- ✿ Be aware that pets may be a problem.
- ✿ Wash cuddly toys regularly and put them in the deep freeze overnight to kill dust mites.
- ✿ Avoid smoking and pollution, which are irritants and triggers.

BACK

Our backs are under considerable strain every day, and can easily jar or become overtired. Avoid vigorous exercise and do not put undue strain on your back. Instead:

- Warm up before exercising.
- Watch your weight.
- Bend your knees rather than your back when lifting.
- Swim and practise yoga regularly (*see p15*).
- Look after your stomach muscles (*see p127*).
- Sleep on a firm mattress with one supportive pillow.
- Sleep on your side with your legs bent, one over the other, and stretch gently before you get out of bed.
- Make sure your office chair and car seat support you and are at the correct height.
- If you do have back problems, consult an osteopath, chiropractor, physiotherapist or Alexander practitioner.

Low Back Stretcher
A good exercise for stretching the lower back and the hamstrings:

1   Sit on the floor with your left leg out in front, toes up,
    with the leg swung over as far as possible to the left.
2   Bend your right knee and bring your right heel in
    close to the crotch, keeping the left knee flat on
    the floor and holding your left hand in the small
    of your back.
3   Sitting up as straight as possible, twist to the left until
    you are facing the outstretched left leg.
4   Reach out your hand and try to touch your left
    toes, bending from the hips. Bounce up and down
    to loosen the torso, working up to 100 bounces.

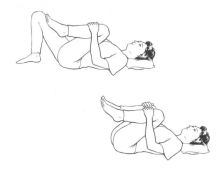

Knee–Chest Stretch

1 Lie on your back on the floor with your knees bent
   and feet 12 inches apart. Place a pillow under your
   head.
2 Take your right knee in your right hand and pull
   towards your chest, bouncing it towards you
   20–50 times.
3 Repeat with the other knee.
4 Pull both knees close to the chest and hold for
   10 seconds.

BAD BREATH

'The distilled water of the floures of Rosemary being drunk at morning and evening first and last, taketh away the stench of the mouth and breath.'
John Gerard, English Renaissance herbalist

Mouthwashes are not the answer. Instead, address the following:

- Maintain good oral hygiene.
- Gargle and snuff a little water into your nose to clear mucus-laden tubes.
- Visit the dentist regularly to deal with decay and cavities.
- Take plenty of calcium and vitamin C to help strengthen teeth and gums.
- Eat live yogurt and parsley, and drink fenugreek or peppermint tea.
- See a nutritionist to check for digestive problems.

'A hot bath! I cry as I sit down in it; and again as I lie flat, a hot bath! How exquisite a vespertime pleasure, how luxurious, fervid and flagrant a consolation for the rigours, the austerities, the renunciations of the day.'

Rose Macaulay

BATHS

Bathing has been associated with relaxation, pampering and indulgence for centuries. For the Egyptians and Romans it was something of an art form, and today's spas are inspired largely by them. Make your bathroom a mini-Sanctuary. Light candles, burn fragrant oils and listen to soothing music whilst you sink into a warm bath and unwind. The Sanctuary CD contains over an hour of relaxing classical music to soothe and restore you. To complete the experience, try one of these home-made blends:

Cornflower Bath Vinegar
Fill a large screw-cap jar with cornflower heads, pour on boiling white vinegar and leave to steep for two weeks, occasionally shaking the jar. Pour one capful of the blue liquid into your bath for an invigorating soak.

Chamomile and Mustard Tonic Bath
Simmer 8 tbs of dried camomile flowers in 2 pints of water. Leave to steep for 1 hour, strain and stir 8 level tbs

of mustard powder into the liquid until dissolved. Pour 1 pint into a bath for easing the first signs of colds and flu.

Honeyed Milk Soak
Stir 1lb of honey into ¹/₂ pint of boiling water in a pan. Add 1¹/₂ pints of milk and whisk. Dissolve 8 tbs of kitchen salt and 2 tbs of bicarbonate of soda in ³/₄ pint of boiling water. Add the two together and shake. This is both an excellent body rub for ridding the body of dead cells and a soothing, nourishing soak.

Neutral Baths
A wonderful way to relax and ease insomnia. A bath thermometer is required as the water should match your body temperature (no more than 36.1ºC/ 97ºF). Immerse yourself in the bath for about 10 minutes, supporting your head so you feel comfortable. Ideally you should have a neutral bath just before you go to bed.

Essential Oil Bath
See Aromatherapy p11, for recommended oils.

BEAUTY

'Nothing we wear makes as much difference as the expression on our faces.'

Looking good contributes to our overall sense of well-being. Beauty comes from within. When we are in good health, eating wholesome, nutritious food, taking regular exercise, sleeping well and getting fresh air we will naturally enjoy the benefits of clear, glowing skin, shining hair and bright eyes. Good posture, effective breathing, positive thinking and a good skin-care routine are also key ingredients. While some people may have been dealt the trump cards when it comes to looks, they may have been short-changed in other areas! Some people turn heads just by the force of their personality and strong self-image. Beautiful people are warm, generous, confident and full of vitality.

BODY FACTS

In one 24-hour day, on average:

- ♥ Your heart beats 103,689 times.
- ♥ Your nails grow .000046 inches.
- ♥ Your hair grows .01714 inches.
- ♥ You eat 3¾lb of food.
- ♥ You lose 7–8 lb of waste.
- ♥ You turn in your sleep 24 to 35 times.
- ♥ You move 750 major muscles.
- ♥ You breathe 23,640 times.
- ♥ You inhale 438 cubic feet of air.
- ♥ You drink 2.9 lb of liquids.
- ♥ You perspire 1.43 pints.
- ♥ You exercise 7,000,000 brain cells.
- ♥ You speak 4,800 words.

BREATHING

One of the best ways to calm your mind and promote healing in your body is to breathe properly. Not as easy as it sounds, and most of us survive on shallow, quick breaths which do not enable the all-important oxygen to reach our bloodstream effectively. The key to breathing is to allow your diaphragm to rise and fall, not your chest.

1 Lie down on a bed wearing loose clothing.
2 Place one hand on your chest and the other on your abdomen.
3 Breathe in slowly through your nose to the count of 10 – your abdomen should rise.
4 Breathe out slowly through your mouth making a 'HER' or 'AAH' sound – your abdomen should fall gently.
5 Repeat this exercise 15 times, and as often as you can during the day, whether lying, sitting or standing.

BUTTOCKS

'A pair of firm, nicely rounded buttocks can really enhance the figure.'

Bharti Vyas

I once saw a great street poster which showed a woman with a 'Marilyn Monroe' type bottom walking along a road, and underneath it simply stated 'Turn your Wobble into a Wiggle'. What a great ad: I wished I had thought of it!

To firm up your buttocks clench them whenever you remember, including while you are standing at the basin and when you are walking. You can also try this exercise regularly:

1 Tighten your buttock muscles and pinch firmly all over your bottom.
2 Hold for a count of ten, then release.
3 Repeat 30 times.

CALCIUM

A calcium deficiency can cause weakened bones and teeth, plus poor blood clotting, insomnia and high blood pressure.

Sources include: dairy foods, dark green leafy vegetables, nuts, seeds and sardines.

Increase your intake of vegetables and fish rich in calcium if you are menopausal or pregnant. With an increase in nut intolerance it may be advisable not to eat nuts, particularly peanuts, whilst pregnant, and results of recent studies indicate that an excess amount of dairy products may contribute to osteoporosis.

CELLULITE

Cellulite is thought to be caused by a build-up of toxins, and is more common in women than in men.

There are some excellent treatments now available which address localized fat and cellulite, including hydro-therapy, body scrubs, and a variety of body wraps*. By stimulating the circulation, increasing lymph drainage and assisting with the elimination of toxins they help break down cellulite. A course of treatments, plus the following self-help measures, is recommended.

- ⚘ Avoid caffeine, chocolate, fizzy drinks and alcohol; drink herbal teas and plenty of water instead.
- ⚘ Reduce refined starches, sugars and packaged foods.
- ⚘ Eat plenty of raw vegetables, fruit and parsley.
- ⚘ Blend celery and cucumber juice for a healthy 'eliminator' drink which also aids kidney function.
- ⚘ Massage the area with a blend of juniper berry, cypress, patchouli and rosemary oils (3 drops of each in a carrier oil).
- ⚘ Use of a massage glove or loofah in the shower is also effective in waking up circulation, as are alternate splashes of cold and hot water in the shower.
- ⚘ Exercise vigorously for at least 20 minutes three times a week – the increased circulation will help clear tissues of their toxic sludge as well as toning up muscles after loss of fat.

* available at The Sanctuary

CHINESE MEDICINE

In China, many centuries ago, patients paid their physicians only when they were well: if they became ill, he was not treating them correctly. There is a lot of merit in this approach to medicine, and it is interesting that many people today are turning to Chinese medicine and other complementary systems to help them achieve a better state of health. Chinese medicine encompasses acupuncture, acupressure and herbalism, and uses many diagnostic techniques that are unfamiliar to Western practitioners. It is particularly useful in treating stubborn conditions such as asthma, infertility and skin problems that orthodox medicine has failed to cure.

CLOTHES

It is all too easy to be tempted into buying the latest styles and colours without focusing on what really suits us. Be aware of your body shape and the most flattering styles for you, your skin, eye and hair tones and which colours enhance your looks. There are plenty of colour, style and wardrobe consultants, but before buying anything, stop and think:

- Will this 'go' with other clothes I have?
- How many times a year will I wear it and is it therefore worth the price?
- Although the sales person says it's me, does it *really* flatter me in terms of design, cut and colour?
- Do I feel comfortable in it: is it perhaps too young, old, long, short, loose or tight?
- How easy is it to clean and how crease-resistant is it?

COLOUR

Since ancient times the importance of colour in healing has been recognized. Each colour vibrates at a different frequency, while white is a mixture of many different wavelengths. Colour affects us profoundly, for not just our eyes, but the cells in our bodies respond to light and colour, and indeed chromotherapy is now used not only by alternative practitioners but also in hospitals where it is used for its effect on the emotions of mentally ill patients and to enhance the growth of premature babies. Although I believe that for different people different colours can have a different effect, there is substantial research that links certain colours with various health problems.

Use these healing colours in your life by wearing them, using them in interior design, by imagining or visualizing the colours, or even by eating them as foods.

- *Red*: for anaemia, low blood pressure, headaches and colds.
- *Orange:* for bronchitis, lower back pain, painful periods and healing after childbirth.
- *Yellow:* helps the liver and intestines.
- *Green:* for ulcers, anxiety, headaches and flu.
- *Blue:* for reducing fever, for insomnia, shock and throat problems.
- *Turquoise:* boosts the immune system.
- *Violet:* for kidney and bladder problems and rheumatism.

'The touch of the sea is sensuous, enfolding the body
in its soft, close embrace.'

Kate Chopin

DEAD SEA SALTS

For centuries the health benefits of a soak in the Dead Sea have been legendary. Although no substitute for the real thing, you can still benefit in your home from the properties of the Dead Sea salts (available from health food shops). A long warm (but not hot) bath in Dead Sea salts encourages elimination of waste through the skin's pores, reduces fluid retention, smooths the skin and eases anxiety and stress. If you suffer from eczema or psoriasis use only a small amount until your skin becomes used to the effect. The Sanctuary has recently launched a range of spa products including a Dead Sea salts scrub.

The first Sanctuary abroad opens in early 1999, right on the edge of the Dead Sea in Jordan, and within a few hours' drive of the magnificent Petra.

'Eat, drink and be merry ... for tomorrow we diet.'

'Take what you want and pay for it.'

Spanish proverb

DIETING

Many of us seem to be constantly on a stop, start, stop diet, feeling guilty about eating, or miserable about not eating. We need to get this in perspective. Either we are unhealthily overweight, or we are simply concerned about how we look. I believe it is better to be a little over the weight you would ideally like to be, and happy, than to be thin but deprived.

If you want to lose weight, eat less, eat healthy foods, and exercise. To get the best out of meals and avoid overeating take the following simple steps:

- Sit down while you eat – but not in front of the television, so you are aware of what you are eating.
- Savour each mouthful, and chew it slowly.
- Don't buy tempting high calorie foods: if you don't have the foods in the house it is difficult to eat them!
- Keep healthy snacks to hand (celery, carrots, fruit).
- Use smaller plates so that the portions look bigger and present food attractively.

- ❦ Start with a small portion and when you have finished have extra if you really need it.
- ❦ We need 40 vitamins, minerals and chemicals each day – so eat a balanced diet.
- ❦ Cut out sugar and cut down on fat, salt and protein.
- ❦ Drink water regularly throughout the day.
- ❦ If you are being entertained, let your host know if you wish to avoid certain foods or simply request smaller portions.
- ❦ If you over-indulge one day, eat lightly but healthily the next.
- ❦ Find ways other than food and drink to reward yourself: have a massage or visit a cinema or museum.

We all too easily equate slim bodies with healthy bodies. While it is true that too much weight and fat puts pressure on the heart, circulation and joints, you should be aware of the optimum weight for your body type rather than aiming for an unrealistically thin silhouette.

If you do need to lose weight, do it *slowly*, with a nutritious diet and exercise programme. Don't become fanatical.

DOCTORS

Doctors are very busy people. Gone are the days of the old-style family doctor who seemed to call whenever you needed him\her, who usually knew your parents and family history and early in the appointment would check your pulse, tongue and eyes to assess your general health. Today doctors spend time accessing your file on computer and are under pressure to complete a consultation in 5–10 minutes. To get the most out of your relationship with your doctor and the best for your health:

- Make the effort to become more knowledgeable about your health and have a good reference book at home.
- Let your doctor know you only want to take pills when they are thought absolutely necessary.
- Give positive feedback to your doctor – everyone likes to know that they are appreciated.
- If you cannot get on with your doctor, remember you have the right to change to another doctor.

EATING DISORDERS

The way we feel about ourselves and our bodies is reflected in our attitude towards food. Some eat for comfort; others obsessively starve themselves or binge and vomit. It is very difficult for outsiders to understand the compulsions that lead their loved ones to abuse their bodies with food. It is very important that people with eating disorders seek professional help as soon as possible.

EVENING PRIMROSE OIL

Evening Primrose Oil contains gamma linolenic acid, essential for cell regeneration, immunity and balance of the nervous system. GLA is necessary for balanced hormone production and therefore helps prevent the symptoms of pre-menstrual tension and painful periods. GLA also helps keep skin supple and is a natural anti-inflammatory, so may be useful in arthritic conditions. It is taken as a supplement.

EXCUSES

*'A lot of people lose their health trying to become
wealthy, then lose their wealth trying to become
healthy.'*

It's not enough just to buy exercise equipment, a juicer
and a calorie-counter – you need to motivate yourself to
use them. There will always be excuses not to exercise, not
to eat healthily, and not to watch your weight – but these
are never *reasons*. Being aware of your own procrastina-
tion is half the battle: if you see the changes you want to
effect in your life as a *favour* you are doing yourself rather
than a punishment you will feel more inspired. Sometimes
it helps to write down all your excuses and then eliminate
them one by one, replacing them with positive statements
to support your goals. (*See Affirmations and Visualization*
in *Treasures from the Sanctuary for the Mind*).

EXERCISE

'If you don't use it, you lose it.'

*'I wouldn't dream of starting the day until I have
taken my morning dose of youth elixir – exercise.'*
Ginger Rogers, aged 60

We tend to feel that our lives are too busy to fit in a regular
exercise routine. Think again: all you need is 20 minutes,
at least three times a week (the aim is to break into a sweat),
but if you are just starting 10 minutes a day will get you
going! I believe in health-related fitness rather than fitness
for fitness' sake or for building bulging muscles. Getting
the balance right is Important, and the benefits of regular,
safe, balanced exercise can include:

- improved digestion
- increased stamina, strength and suppleness – important to maintain as we get older
- clearer and more creative thinking
- improved appearance
- increased protection against circulatory and heart disease, arthritis and osteoporosis
- reduced cholesterol
- enhanced immune system and increased vitality
- reduced depression and insomnia.

Choose from dancing, tennis, jogging, rebounding, cycling, aerobics and the gentler methods of yoga, walking, swimming and t'ai chi. Weight-bearing exercise is good for guarding against osteoporosis. If you find a form of exercise you like you'll be more motivated to continue. Remember exercise can be done with a friend or family member, maximizing your rewards from the time invested.

EYE CARE

Your eyes are precious and must be treated with great care. A regular check-up at the optician's is advisable: not only can he/she pick up if you need glasses or contact lenses, but also if you have any serious eye disorders. Glaucoma, which can lead to blindness if untreated, can occur in children but is most common over the age of 40. Eyes can become sore and reddened through fatigue or pollution, but do not administer any drops yourself before consulting a professional. The skin around your eyes is delicate and should not be pulled or rubbed.

For Tired Eyes
Place 2 chamomile tea bags in hot distilled water. When lukewarm, remove tea bags, squeeze out and place on closed eyes. Rest for 15 minutes. Alternatively, cut slices from a fresh cucumber and rest with a slice over each eye.

FACIAL MASSAGE

For toning muscles, draining away toxins and adding a healthy glow to your face:

1 Apply a very light film of massage oil to your face.
2 With your thumbs beneath your chin and the balls of your fingers on top, pinch along the jawbone to the earlobes. Repeat ten times.
3 Press the balls of the first two fingers of each hand along the underside of the cheekbones, gently pressing and releasing. Work towards the outside, then towards the centre, repeating ten times.
4 Using the balls of your index fingers, apply pressure to the muscles on either side of the nose, starting at the bridge and moving down to the nostrils. Continue for one minute.
5 Close your eyes. Use your third fingers to trace all around the bony rims of the eye sockets, very gently. Repeat ten times.

6 Place your thumbs on the outside edge of your
   eyebrows and your index fingers just above the inner
   edge. Pinch the skin lightly up towards the hairline
   and back again.

FACIAL SKIN CARE ROUTINE

Your daily routine should be:

1 Cleanse: using a facial wash, or lotion if your skin is dry. Cold-pressed oil such as almond is good for older skins – rub in gently using upward movements, then remove with damp cotton wool.
2 Tone: use a toner suited to your skin type to remove all traces of cleansing lotion. Cold water splashed on the face is an excellent 'toner' for dry skins.
3 Moisturize: apply your choice of cream to damp skin to seal in moisture. There are many excellent creams: the aim is to prevent water from evaporating from the skin and drying it out.
4 Gently exfoliate once a week with a shop-bought cream. Exfoliation is better avoided if you are prone to broken veins.
5 A visit to a qualified and experienced beauty therapist is a worthwhile investment to establish the best regime for your skin type.

FACIAL TREATMENTS

Cleanse your face and apply the following natural face masks when your skin needs a boost. Remove by splashing with cool water and pat dry.

Revitalizing Barley Mask
Mix together: 2 tbs powdered barley, 2 tsp fresh chopped mint, 2 tbs clear honey and 2–3 tbs full fat milk.

Fresh Fruit Mask
Mash together: ½ ripe avocado, 1 tbs fresh tomato juice, 1 tbs lemon juice.

Refreshing Facial Spritzer
Mix 1 tbs witch hazel and 5 drops of your favourite essential oil. Leave in a closed container overnight. Add ¾ cup distilled water and pour into a spray bottle. Shake well before using and close eyes before spraying.

FASTING

'When one feeds a sick person, one only feeds the illness.'

Hippocrates

'At a dinner party one should eat wisely but not too well, and talk well but not too wisely.'

Oscar Wilde

It has long been recognized that properly controlled fasting is an effective way of assisting the body's self-healing abilities, eliminating toxins and improving immune system function. Indeed, Champneys health farm was one of the first places in the UK to pioneer a 'fasting cure' and it has since been discovered that those with diseases such as diabetes, epilepsy, heart disease, colitis and high blood pressure can benefit from supervised fasting. If you are healthy but in need of a detox, short fasts of one or two days can be done at home. People who fast regularly claim to have clearer skin, brighter eyes and more energy.

Water-only fast

1 The day before, eat only fruit and vegetables.
2 Drink between 3 and 6 pints of hot pure water a day, sipping constantly.
3 Relax and keep warm. Do not exercise vigorously, take hot baths or supplements.
4 You may feel dizzy or headachy or on edge: this is to be expected during detoxification.
5 Avoid driving.
6 Go for a gentle walk, watch a funny video, listen to some beautiful music or read something uplifting.
7 The day after, drink diluted fruit juice and homemade vegetable broth slowly and thereafter introduce healthy, wholesome solid foods gradually.

There are many other ways of fasting, including fresh juice-only fasts (*see Juicing p72*), herbal tea fasts, mono-diets (where, for example, one single fruit such as apple is eaten), or much reduced cleansing diets where salads, rice, fruit and vegetables are eaten. Before embarking on a fast, it is wise to discuss it with your health-care provider.

FATIGUE

Extreme tiredness or low spirits may be caused by a variety of problems, including illness, anaemia, low blood sugar or pregnancy, and appropriate checks should be taken with your physician and a nutritionist. The following practical steps can be taken for general fatigue:

✿ Go to bed early and rise early, with good quality sleep in between.

✿ Set achievable goals for each day. Look at your workload and responsibilities objectively: you may need to learn the art of delegation.

✿ Start the day with a nutritious breakfast.

✿ Eat plenty of complex carbohydrates, avoiding refined ('white') carbohydrates.

✿ If you are vegetarian or vegan, ensure you are having sufficient protein.

✿ Avoid sugar, chocolate, caffeine and alcohol, which all give you a sudden rush of energy then leave you lethargic and drowsy.

- Pace yourself, and become aware of the times when you are most productive.
- Embark on a regular exercise programme, starting slowly and building up gradually. Try sociable sports such as badminton.
- Mind, body, spirit exercises such as yoga can have both a calming and an energizing effect.
- Seek the company of positive, fun people as they can nurture and energize you.
- Spend some time outdoors each day benefiting from daylight and fresh air, and do the breathing exercises on p23.
- Wear warm clothing, rather than having the central heating on high.
- Feng shui, colour therapy and crystals may also help create a more energizing environment for you.

FIGHT OR FLIGHT

When they encountered a stressful situation, our primitive ancestors' bodies would prepare them to fight the aggressor, or take flight from it. Threats, circumstances and social behaviour are very different today, but our bodies don't know that, and when faced with stress we still produce adrenalin which causes sweating, a need to urinate, an increase in our breathing rate and a release of sugars and fats into the bloodstream. All very useful when we needed to look fierce, run fast and have blood that clots easily if wounded, but not very helpful when the boss reads the riot act or our neighbours are annoying us.

If we allow ourselves to get stressed over long periods of time on a regular basis it will start to do serious damage to our bodies, putting us at greater risk of heart disease, strokes and other serious illnesses. (*See Stress p123 for how to deal with these situations.*)

'Don't fight, don't flee ... instead learn to flow.'

FREE RADICALS

Free radicals are highly reactive substances that create abnormal chemical bonds in the body's tissues, causing damage throughout the body from wrinkles and premature ageing to degenerative diseases such as cancer. They are taken into the body in the form of pollutants, ultraviolet radiation, smoking and fried or charred food.

- ○ Increase your intake of the 'antioxidant' vitamins A, C and E, plus selenium and zinc. Antioxidants 'mop up' free radicals, preventing them from damaging body cells. Good sources are purple, red and yellow fruit and vegetables.
- ○ Use a high factor sunscreen when in the sun and a moisturizer containing sunscreen for everyday use.
- ○ Take regular exercise and learn stress-reduction techniques to boost your immune system.

FRUIT AND VEGETABLES

Fruit and vegetables are high in vitamins, minerals, fibre, antioxidants and enzymes, and protect against cancer and heart disease.

Always include a wide variety of fruit and vegetables in your diet. You are strongly recommended to eat a minimum of five and up to ten servings per day. The fresher the better: with foods travelling from the far corners of the world and being stored for long periods during transit, in the shops and in our fridges, many of the nutrients have disappeared by the time we eat them.

If you have a garden, consider growing some of your own fruit and vegetables and eating them soon after they are picked. Eat one raw meal a day and when you do cook fruit or vegetables steam them lightly or stir-fry them.

HAIR

'Only God, my dear
Could love you for yourself alone
And not your yellow hair.'

W. B. Yeats

Hair grows from follicles, each follicle being supplied with nutrients and oxygen by the blood vessels. The average scalp sprouts no fewer than 120,000 hairs, 50–100 of which are shed each day to make way for new growth, with more being shed in autumn or after pregnancy. Stress, poor circulation, thyroid problems, illness, heavy drinking and smoking can cause hair loss, but 75% of men over 40 show some signs of baldness, most of which is hereditary. The following advice may help:

A good diet is essential, especially one rich in raw fruits and dark green leafy vegetables, plenty of water and limited junk food. Hair is protein, so a regular intake of fish, eggs, and white meat is advisable.

- Vitamin B complex is particularly important. It is found in brewer's yeast, yogurt, wheatgerm, black treacle, liver, wholemeal bread, milk, kidneys and brown rice.
- Nutritionists also recommend vitamins A, C and D, calcium, iron, zinc, iodine and copper.
- Use a gentle shampoo and concentrate on the roots, using this as an opportunity to massage your scalp. Use only a small amount of conditioner and rinse thoroughly. Gently pat dry, and only start to blow dry when it is almost dry.
- Regular scalp massage with a little coconut oil will stimulate the blood flow to the hair and in turn will encourage lustrous, thick growth. You will need to wash your hair twice afterwards to remove all noticeable traces of the oil. In fact, if you do this regularly, some oil will remain to condition and protect your hair.

Natural Hair Conditioners

1. *Egg and Olive Oil:* Whisk up 2 tbs olive oil, 1 egg yolk and 1 tbs cider vinegar. Massage the ingredients into your hair and leave for at least 30 minutes, wrapped in a warm towel. Shampoo your hair and rinse thoroughly.

2. *Yogurt:* Mix together 6 tbs natural yogurt and 1 egg. After shampooing and rinsing, massage the ingredients into your hair for 4 minutes. Wrap your hair in a warm towel and leave for 10 minutes. Rinse well with tepid water.

HEADACHES

Most headaches are caused by tension in the neck, shoulders and forehead muscles. You tense up involuntarily for a variety of reasons: a poorly positioned VDU, too much noise, concentration, eye strain and emotional problems. Persistent headaches should be checked by a doctor, and osteopaths, chiropractors and acupuncturists may be able to help, but home remedies include the following:

- Learn a relaxation technique.
- Drink a cup of chamomile tea, or place a few drops of Rescue Remedy on your tongue.
- Swirl lavender oil into a warm bath or massage 2 drops into the temples.
- Relax neck muscles with a hot water bottles.
- Avoid sugary or caffeine-rich foods.
- Have a shoulder, neck or head massage, which you can do yourself.
- Watch your posture and avoid carrying heavy items.
- Eliminate foods to which you are allergic.

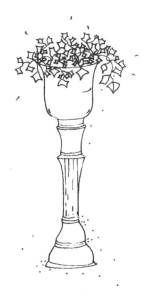

'Let your food be your medicine; let your medicine be your food.'

Hippocrates

HEALTHY EATING

Healthy eating does not have to be sackcloth and ashes, nor does it have to be carrot juice and lettuce leaves. Foods that are wholesome and have a high nutritional content can be as delicious as they are good for us. Many health resorts around the world now offer some of the best dining experiences available. Instead of eating junk foods and resorting to yo-yo dieting, we need to take a fresh look at eating for life.

- Spend your money on quality rather than quantity.
- Shop regularly so your food is fresh.
- Read the labels: take the freshest produce and avoid foods with colouring, flavouring, preservatives and other additives.
- Eat one raw meal a day and plenty of fresh fruit and vegetables.
- Organically grown foods are preferable.
- Wash all fresh fruit and vegetables before eating.
- Eat a balanced diet with a wide variety of food.

- Avoid sugary products.
- Reduce salt, saturated fat and refined produce.
- Moderate your intake of animal protein, particularly red meat.
- Use attractive crockery and make an effort to present food well, even if you are eating alone.
- Eat slowly and chew your food well.
- Steam rather than boil, grill rather than fry, and bake rather than roast.
- Check for any food intolerances you may have.
- If you are considering supplements a nutrition consultation is advisable.

HERBAL TEAS

Think seriously about drinking these instead of caffeine-rich tea and coffee. Caffeine produces a burst of adrenalin output in the body, disturbing the body's equilibrium and using up much-needed energy. It also upsets the pancreas, increasing insulin output and makes you retain water (and put on weight).

There are some lovely varieties of herbal teas now available including:

- peppermint for digestion and congested headaches
- lime flower or chamomile for insomnia and to calm the mind
- vervain for energy and 'verve' in the morning
- borage: good if you're feeling down in the dumps
- thyme for chest complaints and insomnia.

HIGH BLOOD PRESSURE

It is a good idea to have your blood pressure checked annually. Many people have high blood pressure for some time before it is diagnosed. To maintain healthy blood pressure:

♥ Eat oily fish such as sardines, salmon and mackerel.
♥ Eat more soluble fibre such as fruit and vegetables.
♥ Reduce coffee, salt, sugar, fat and red meat consumption.
♥ Stop smoking and moderate alcohol intake to one or two units maximum per day – red wine seems preferable.
♥ Lose weight if you need to.
♥ Take regular exercise suited to your health and fitness status.
♥ Learn a relaxation technique.
♥ A regular massage can be very beneficial.
♥ Learn and use the breathing exercise on p23.
♥ Hypnotherapy can help to reduce blood pressure.
♥ Get a pet and stroke it.

HOMOEOPATHY

This treatment approach is based on the principle that 'like cures like', or the Law of Similars as enunciated by Dr Samuel Hahnemann, the 19th century German physician. In the past homoeopaths would have first trained in orthodox medicine, but now an increasing number of therapists have not been to medical school. One of the key differences from orthodox medicine is the thoroughness of the history taking, where there is much more emphasis on the psychological as well as physiological make up of the individual and their lifestyle, rather than on the disease they may be suffering from. The British Royal family are known to be advocates of homoeopathy. Self-help 'first aid' kits are now widely available, but there is no substitute for being treated by a qualified and experienced practitioner.

'*One may not doubt that, somehow, good
shall come of water and of mud.*'

Rupert Brooke

HYDROTHERAPY AND SPA
TREATMENTS

In classical times the Romans and Greeks brought pure mountain water into towns via aqueducts, to drink or bathe in, and founded towns around health-giving watering places. There was some debate as to whether it was genuinely good for rheumatic disorders or was simply a self-indulgent waste of time, and the argument persists today.

The waters may be taken externally or internally, and used as a relaxant or stimulant. Water can be used in many forms of treatment including sitz baths, colonic irrigation, Scots douche, salt rubs, thalassotherapy and hydrotherapy baths containing essential oils (or seaweed, epsom salts or mud). Many of these treatments have been popular for decades in health resorts and are now available to a wider public in day spas which have become very popular in recent times.

HYPNOTHERAPY

Contrary to popular belief, the role of the hypnotherapist is not to impose his/her own will upon you, but to empower you to achieve your own conscious desire to be well. There is probably no other therapy which more dramatically permits a person to 'take control' of his or her own health than hypnosis. There are two main types of hypnotherapy. The first puts patients into a trance and suggests that their symptoms will disappear; the second uses the trance to facilitate whatever form of psychological treatment is being used, for example, to enable the therapist to explore the subconscious mind.

One can learn and use self-hypnotherapy to deal with many disorders including high blood pressure, asthma, migraine, insomnia, ulcers and addictions. Post-hypnotic suggestion cannot break addiction on its own, but it can help tide addicts over the difficult stage when craving is at its height. Hypnosis can also be effective in pain control, childbirth and phobias.

IRON

An iron deficiency can cause anaemia, depression, lethargy, mouth ulcers and brittle nails.

Sources include fish, poultry, red meat, beetroot, molasses, beans, pulses and dark green leafy vegetables.

If you suspect you are deficient, see your doctor for a blood test: you may be prescribed a supplement.

JUICING

Fresh, raw fruit and vegetable juices are an extremely effective way of taking in large amounts of nutrients and can be highly cleansing and detoxifying. If you remove the fibre (pulp) from the juice you will still need to eat fresh fruit and vegetables to obtain the required amount of roughage in your diet. Some fruits are associated with the natural treatment of certain conditions:

Cranberry juice: for cystitis
Celery juice: for fluid retention
Leafy green vegetable juice: for neutralizing toxins in
    the gut
Papaya and carrot juice: for digestive problems
Pears: for allergies

Try these delicious blends.

- ○ *Strawberry Fair:* 4fl oz/115ml strawberry juice and 4fl oz/115ml mango juice.
- ○ *Top Grape:* 5fl oz/145ml grape juice and 3fl oz/80ml pear juice.
- ○ *Apple Soother:* 3fl oz/80ml apple juice, 3fl oz/80ml carrot juice and 2fl oz/50 ml pineapple juice.
- ○ *Blushing Beetroot:* 6fl oz/170ml carrot juice and 2fl oz/50ml beetroot juice.
- ○ *Super Spinach:* 4fl oz/115ml carrot juice, 2fl oz/50ml spinach juice and 2 fl oz/50ml celery juice.

LAUGHTER

When we are happy we are more relaxed, positive and accepting: our lives feel as if they are in balance.

There is a famous story about Norman Cousins who was told by doctors he was terminally ill. He knew about the ill effects of negative thinking and wondered if positive thinking could make him better. So he rented comedy films and read funny stories. He found that laughing relieved pain and enabled him to sleep. And, to the amazement of the medical profession, he recovered fully.

Worry, stress and other forms of suffering can age both our appearance and our health. Fun and laughter have a rejuvenating effect on the body, and laughter is often referred to as 'internal massage' due to its effect of exercising the heart, lungs and nerves. Research has shown that laugher releases the body's own natural pain killers, *endorphins* and *enkephalins*, as well as *cateholamines*, which speed up the healing process. As a result of this research, laughter clinics are springing up around the world, proving that laughter really is the best medicine.

'A merry heart doth good like medicine, but a broken spirit dryeth up the bones.'

Proverbs 17:22

'If we make ourselves smile, we actually feel like smiling.'

Alfred Adler

'A pain is a cry for help.'

'We have been given two ears: one ear for the sounds around us; one ear for the sound of the still, small voice within us.'

Oriental proverb

LISTEN ... TO YOUR BODY

Our bodies do send out SOS signals, signs that all is not well, and change and action are required to avert a potentially serious problem. We often tend to ignore these warning signs, saying things like 'I don't have time to be ill.' Of course this is not true, and you may be forced to lie down and accept it! Respond to your body's initial, often gentle, pleas for help and be kind to yourself. There is a high price to pay for handing over the responsibility for our health ... or ignoring it.

- ✿ Take the time to learn how your body functions and how to take care of it.
- ✿ Sit down for 5 minutes at the end of the day in a quiet room.
- ✿ Go within yourself, and try to build a relationship with your lungs, heart, stomach and liver: listen to how they are feeling. Are you tired, sad, anxious?
- ✿ Take ten deep breaths and resolve to take action about whatever signs you have detected.

LOVE YOUR BODY

We have become used to criticizing our own bodies for their perceived imperfections. We say we 'hate' our thighs, our upper arms, our chin, our nose, our breasts, our legs ... Stop for a moment. How often have you heard someone say something similar about herself and you genuinely cannot see what she means? Attaining model-like perfection is an unhealthy modern obsession and can only lead to misery: indeed it has been a strong contributor to the increase in eating disorders. The most beautiful people are those whose beauty shines from within, whose characters, not bodies, represent how the outside world sees them.

♥ Decide to stop hating your body or any parts of it.
♥ Follow a healthy lifestyle and be thankful for your body's health.
♥ Even if it seems strange, tell yourself you love those parts of your body you used to dislike.
♥ Go to the gym, have massages and pamper yourself.

10-MINUTE MAKEOVER

1 Cleanse, tone and moisturize before applying make-up.

2 Use a green-tinted cream to tone down any blotches, and put concealer on spots.

3 Apply foundation with a sponge. Blend into jawline with the dry side of the sponge. Test foundation for colour on your *face*: it should disappear into your skin.

4 'Set' foundation with loose powder.

5 Use a light colour eyeshadow on entire eye area up to the eyebrow and apply a medium colour from the outside corner to the middle of the eyelid.

6 With a darker colour, apply a line just above the eye itself and blend with the first light colour.

7 Underline the eye from the corner to the middle with a dark pencil.

8 Apply blusher with a large brush, starting at the hairline and coming diagonally down towards the nose.

9 Outline your lips with a lip pencil, then apply a lighter colour lipstick.

10 Apply mascara last to avoid smudges.

MANICURE

1 Remove all traces of old polish with remover and cotton wool.
2 File nails with an emery board, in one direction only.
3 Massage cuticle cream into the base of each nail.
4 Soak hands in soapy water and clean under the nails with an orange stick wrapped in cotton wool.
5 Apply cuticle remover and push cuticles back with an orange stick.
6 Cut away dead skin with cuticle clippers.
7 Rinse hands and apply lotion. Wipe off excess.
8 Apply base coat to nails and allow to dry.
9 Apply polish to the nails on one hand, allow to dry then apply to the other hand.
10 Repeat.
11 Apply top coat and allow to dry for 15 minutes.

If your nails are in poor condition a professional manicure is a worthwhile investment.

MASSAGE

Massage is as old as history and can be found in every culture in the world in one form or another. The mystery is why, until recently, it should have drifted out of fashion in the West. This was probably due to advances in scientific medicine during the 19th century, which led to a belief that massage would no longer be required and physiotherapists turning to electrical gadgets.

Touch is an essential element of well-being and one of the most instinctive human impulses. An hour's massage by an experienced therapist in a day spa can ease tired muscles, improve circulation and calm the mind.

There are now many books available from which you can learn simple but effective massage movements to carry out on yourself or friends and family: a wonderful giving and receiving experience.

Use cold-pressed oils such as olive oil, jojoba and almond oil, mixed with a few drops of aromatherapy oils if you wish (*see Aromatherapy p11*), set aside some time for yourself and let those tensions flow away.

MILK

Many people find they are intolerant of or allergic to milk products. Milk proteins are difficult to digest and can mean that your body is less able to absorb nutrients. Try cutting out milk, cheese and butter for a month and see how much more healthy you feel. You will be able to take in ample calcium from dark, leafy green vegetables such as spinach and sardines, nuts and sesame seeds.

There are now many milk substitutes available, including rice milk, soya milk and goats' milk.

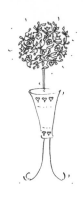

'The mind can make decisions, but so can the heart, so can the hormonal pathways, so can each cell, so can the DNA at the centre of each cell. When they all act in harmony, the result is perfect health and natural, life-enhancing intelligence.'

Deepak Chopra

'The picture of health requires a happy frame of mind.'

MIND—BODY LINK

The 'placebo effect' is a well-documented phenomenon, proving that people who *believe* they are taking something that will cure them are more likely to get well than those who *believe* they taking sugar pills. The implications of this are vast, and we are just starting to learn about the power of the mind to heal the body.

Most complementary therapies take as their starting point the fact that any illness should be treated by treating the whole person, not purely the symptom in question, and this means looking at the mental and emotional state of the patient. The medical profession itself is now starting to acknowledge the importance of this, but I urge you to explore the world of complementary health as well as respecting your GP. We have a health system we cannot afford, and people have to take more responsibility for their own health. Much of what kills us is preventable, and preventative medicine starts with yourself: your body, your mind, and, I believe, your spirit.

'Let us give nature some chance to work; she understands her business better than we. One can exorcise illness better by courtesy than by defiance.'

NATUROPATHY

Three main principles apply. First, that all forms of disease are mainly due to the accumulation in the system of waste materials and bodily refuse which has been steadily piling up in the body through years of unhealthy living habits. Secondly, that the symptoms of all acute diseases are nothing more than the body's attempts to throw off the accumulations of waste material, and suppressing these symptoms with orthodox treatment merely drives them underground, to return another day. The third principle is that the body contains within itself the power to bring about a return to positive health, provided the right methods are employed to help it.

Treatment usually includes: fasting, nutrition, hydrotherapy, body-building, colonic irrigation and psychotherapy. Naturopaths are often also osteopaths, concentrating on the spinal column, which is integral to the bone and muscle system and houses the body's nervous system.

NECK

Neck pain is usually a result of muscle spasm caused by fatigue, poor posture, tension, carrying heavy items, driving, or lack of appropriate support while sleeping.

- Make sure your car seat gives maximum support and your chair is the right height for your VDU.
- Do not hold the phone between your shoulder and your ear and do not drop your head when reading.
- Sleep on your side with one supportive pillow.
- Take moderate exercise once a day.
- Slowly turn your head to the right as far as it will go. Hold for 20 seconds. Turn back to the centre and drop your head slowly to your chest. Turn your head to the left as far as it will go. Hold for 20 seconds. Repeat 3–5 times every 10–15 minutes.
- Alternate hot and cold packs to any painful part of the neck.
- Pay attention to your posture and learn not to tense muscles.

Neck and Shoulder Loosener

1 Stand with feet slightly apart.
2 Bend forward with your arms and head hanging loosely.
3 Bring your arms forward, up and back in a free-swinging circle, or one at a time if that is more comfortable.
4 Do 50–300 circles at least once a day.

NECK BEAUTY

The neck is one of the first areas to display tell-tale signs of ageing, with fleshy rings and a crêpey look gradually appearing. To combat this, cleanse and moisturize well, and massage regularly:

1 Once a week, with a little oil, massage the neck from left to right in an upward-stroking motion, one hand following the other.
2 After three minutes pinch the front and sides of the neck gently, using your right hand for the left side and vice versa.
3 Finish with an additional two minutes of stroking.

Honey Throat Cream:
Mix together 2½ tbs runny honey, 2½ tsp olive oil and 2 egg yolks. Cover and leave for 24 hours in the fridge before smoothing onto your neck. Tissue off after 20 minutes, then gently rinse with warm water using cotton wool.

NURTURE

I have been in the nurturing business for over 30 years and love it. It is wonderful to know that the work you do is of special benefit to others. There are very few businesses where staff are in such intimate contact with clients, spending on average an hour in a private room, using their hands, minds and hearts to relax, heal and nurture the body, mind and spirit.

I recently had the most nurturing and giving experience I have ever received in terms of spa treatment where I was held, cradled, moved and massaged in water for nearly three hours.

Nurture is one of the most beautiful gifts to give and receive. Sadly many people believe they are too busy for either. If this is you, make a pledge to change from today. It can add years to your life and life to your years.

> *'One must first care for oneself, so that one can then dare care for someone else.'*
>
> Maya Angelou

'Let your food be your medicine; let your medicine be your food.'

Hippocrates

NUTRITIONAL HEALING

Nutritional healing is much more than following government guidelines for healthy eating. Environmental pollutants and the use of drugs such as antibiotics cause changes in our bodies which affect their ability to absorb nutrients. Chronic illnesses such as bad skin, digestive problems, hyperactivity, headaches and chronic fatigue may result. However, complementary practitioners and, increasingly, some orthodox medical professionals are looking at what people are eating and what, if any, nutritional supplements are required.

It may be possible to treat yourself with information gleaned from books, but often the individual and the ailment are so complex it is worth consulting a nutritional therapist.

OSTEOPATHY

*'Osteopathy is concerned with the establishment
and maintenance of the normal structural integrity
of the body.'*

Dr Alan Stoddard

This structural integrity is achieved primarily through
manipulation of joints in order to restore them to their
normal positions and mobility, thereby relieving abnormal tension in muscles and ligaments.

We can learn from our pets. All animals gently stretch
after sleep, arching and then hollowing out their spinal
columns so that the vertebrae are given the opportunity
to 'mesh' into the right alignment.

To avoid the need for osteopathy, work on your posture, following the advice given on p99.

PEDICURE

1. Soak your feet in warm soapy water or epsom salts for several minutes.
2. Pat them dry, and rub off hard skin with a pumice stone.
3. Cut your nails square across and smooth the edges with an emery board.
4. Apply cuticle remover and push the cuticles back with an orange stick.
5. Massage cream or body lotion into your feet for several minutes, and wipe off any excess from the nails.
6. Separate your toes with tissues.
7. Apply a base coat to your toe nails and allow to dry.
8. Apply polish and allow to dry.
9. Repeat.
10. Apply top coat and allow to dry for 15 minutes.

To avoid damaging your nails, nail polish is best for special occasions, rather than all the time.

PLASTIC SURGERY

With the amount of media coverage of facelifts, skin peels, breast enhancement, eye and tummy tucks, we may be forgiven for thinking that it is normal for a woman to resort to surgery in an attempt to halt the ageing process and 'improve' on nature. It is not. What *is* normal is regretting the passing of time and the effect it is having on our bodies. Our colouring and shape usually change with age. This could be a great time to invest in a new hairstyle, take a fresh look at our make-up, maybe get some professional advice, and also take a fresh look at our wardrobe, dress style and what colours now suit us best.

Remember our relationships with others are based on personality rather than our looks, so if it is others you want to impress then think again. If it is for your own satisfaction, look at this carefully. There are risks in surgery that can lead to future problems. Having fun and laughing are the most rejuvenating things we can do for our bodies and we should revel in the good qualities that age can bring, such as experience, confidence, grace, depth and wit.

PMS

Symptoms of premenstrual syndrome include depression, irritability, fluid retention, fatigue, weepiness, mood swings, clumsiness, backache and headaches just before the start of a period. Some natural solutions include:

- ❧ vitamin B6, magnesium, zinc and vitamin E supplements (consult a nutritionist for suitable dosages)
- ❧ avoidance of stimulants such as alcohol and coffee
- ❧ regular nutritious meals, avoiding sugar and saturated fat
- ❧ evening primrose oil (take 6 × 500mg capsules daily throughout the cycle)
- ❧ acupuncture and selected herbs, especially *agnus castus* and *dong quai*
- ❧ exercise, which stimulates endorphins and relaxes the muscles
- ❧ if possible, minimize your activities and responsibilities during the time you know you will be suffering.

POSTURE

*'Give me the children at the age of six. They will
learn gymnastics for the balance of the body; they
will learn the arts for the balance of the mind.'*

Plato

Bad posture is the most common crime against the body.
Prior to school, children's posture is usually excellent. Years
of slumping over a desk on an uncomfortable chair, carrying heavy books and being given negative messages by
teachers leads to round shoulders and poor posture. As
mind and body are intimately connected, this can lead to a
variety of conditions, from back pain to migraine. Ensure
when you are sitting that your back is supported and your
spine is upright. High heels will throw your whole body
out of alignment. When walking, feel that you are upright
and well-aligned. Exercise and correct (abdominal) breathing will help build muscle tone and release body tension.
Yoga, Alexander Technique, Rolfing or Heller Work can
all be very useful for improving posture.

PRESCRIPTION DRUGS

'There is no such thing as a free lunch.'

'Your health is your own responsibility.'

It is too easy to prescribe a pill, and it is too easy to swallow one, particularly when we want an instant cure. But every single drug has a side effect, from antibiotics to cocaine. Some side effects are, of course, more serious than others, and some illnesses do require the use of drugs.

Drugs treat the symptom rather than the cause, so if you do need to take drugs as a last resort, take steps to find out the cause of your illness. Make sure you are aware of what you are taking, and before you go to the doctor prepare a list of any questions you may have, plus any information you can give about your condition which may help with the diagnosis. Always ask your doctor:

What exactly is wrong with me? When the doctor gives your condition a name, write it down and if necessary ask him/her to spell it so you can look it up later and gain more knowledge of your illness.

Do I need to take this drug or will the illness get better of its own accord in time: or is there any non-drug way I can deal with the condition?

What are the possible side effects of this drug?

In addition, if you are taking long-term prescription drugs then agree a review date with your doctor. Be aware of the 'use by' dates on your medicines and return out of date drugs to your pharmacist. Always follow the directions given, and drink lots of water during the period you are taking medicinal drugs and for at least a week after you have completed the course. Finally, remember that you do have the right to change your doctor if you are unhappy with him or her.

PROTEIN

Too much protein builds up toxins in the body, puts a burden on the kidneys, is difficult for the digestive system to cope with, and is stored in the body as fat. Excess protein can also make the blood acidic, which can lead to headaches, gout and brittle bone disease. If you do not get enough protein your hair, nails, teeth, skin and muscle condition will suffer. Current advice is that 55 grams a day is the optimum amount, with a small amount at each meal. The best protein to eat is in chicken, eggs, fish, nuts, seeds and pulses. Avoid fatty, red and processed meats.

REFLEXOLOGY

The early Chinese, Japanese, Indians, Russians and Egyptians worked on the feet to promote good health. Today, many of these same techniques have been developed into the method of reflexology, which, like acupuncture, is based on the principle of energy zones running through the body, with reflex areas in the feet that correspond to all the major organs, glands and body parts. By applying a certain type of pressure to specific points on the foot a dynamic healing and relaxation response is achieved. There are some excellent books which make it easy to learn the rudiments of reflexology for home use, but, like all therapies, to treat specific and serious problems an experienced reflexologist should be consulted. However, whenever your feet are tired you can give them a good, relaxing and revitalizing massage yourself. Use hand cream or a few drops of peppermint oil swirled into olive oil, and massage your toes and toenails, paying special attention to the web between the toes. Push your thumb along the dips between the tendons from the top of your foot to the toes, and rub the soles of your feet well. Nicer still if you could do it to a friend and have them return the favour, in which case it is a good idea to start by bathing your feet in warm water.

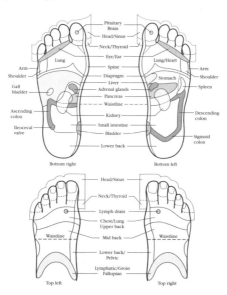

RELAXATION

It is very important that you take time in your day to relax and recharge, even if it is only quiet contemplation on the train to work, a sit in the park during your lunch break or a soak in the bath before retiring. Below are some techniques you might like to try.

Relaxation Exercise I
This breathing exercise encourages toxin release via the lungs and lymphatic system, calms the mind and enhances immune function:

1. Sit with your hands resting between your ribs and your navel.
2. Inhale fully, counting to two.
3. Exhale, counting to six at the same rate.
4. Be aware of your hands rising and falling with your diaphragm.
5. Repeat at least 20 times.

Relaxation Exercise II
This comes from a system called Autogenic Training.

1   Lie on the floor with your eyes closed and, if it is
    more comfortable, with your knees bent.
2   Concentrate on your right arm and say to yourself,
    'My right arm feels heavy.' Imagine it is weighing
    down heavily on the floor.
3   Repeat several times for a minute, then move to
    your left arm, right leg, and left leg feeling them as
    warm and heavy. If you lose focus don't worry, simply
    move your attention back to the limb and continue.
    Go through each limb, right and left.
4   Finish the exercise by focusing on your forehead,
    which feels cool and awake. Clench and unclench
    your fists to bring your senses back to the present
    reality.

Relaxation Exercise III

1 Lie down in a comfortable place.
2 Ensure your body is lying evenly, with your hands by your sides and your palms facing upwards.
3 Close your eyes and feel the stillness.
4 Inhale and exhale fully, feeling your abdomen rise and fall.
5 As you inhale, repeat 'Deep and long and slow', and as you exhale, repeat 'Slow and long and deep'. Notice how your breathing becomes deeper, longer and slower.
6 Feel your inhalations taking in energy and exhalations breathing out stress.
7 After five minutes or so, stir yourself gently.

Relaxation Exercise IV

1 Lie down in a comfortable place.
2 As you breathe in, concentrate on the muscles in
  your forehead and mentally repeat 'relax and let go'.
3 Continue down the body towards your feet, relaxing
  each muscle in turn: neck, shoulders, chest, back,
  stomach and finally feet.

*'Workaholism is the addiction of choice for those
who feel unworthy.'*

*'Remember today is a day for enjoying as well
as doing.'*

SAD

Seasonal Affective Disorder, which affects more women than men, is now recognised as a serious problem during the winter months. It is thought to be connected to a residual human need to hibernate.

The pineal gland is the body's 'light meter' and it is this that affects the body when it is not exposed to sufficient daylight, causing depression and lethargy. With our busy lives it is easy to become house-and office-bound. Make an effort to spend time outdoors in daylight on a daily basis. Formal treatment for SAD is with FSL (full spectrum lighting).

SALT

The body does require salt, but it can usually obtain what it needs from the fruit and vegetables we eat. In normal conditions our bodies only need about a gram a day, whereas most of us eat 20 times more than this, as salt is included in foods such as breakfast cereals, bread, butter and canned or processed food. Too much salt can cause high blood pressure, anxiety and water retention. To reduce your salt intake:

- Avoid salty, 'moreish' snacks.
- Check labels for the salt content of food.
- Don't add extra salt to your cooking and keep the salt mill off the dining table.
- Use herbs and spices for extra flavour.
- Where salt is used, sea salt is preferable.

SELF-ESTEEM

*'The first 30 years we are told to let it all hang out –
then spend the next 30 trying to push it all back in.'*

*'People call me a feminist whenever I express senti-
ments that differentiate me from a doormat or a
prostitute'.*

Rebecca West

*'I am a serene, free, valuable woman, trusting
myself to risk, unconditionally loving myself and
others.'*

Champney's guest

It is important that we become 'self-caring', that we respect our bodies and feel good about the person we are. This contributes to our equilibrium, which in turn positively impacts on our immune system. (*See Treasures from the Sanctuary for the Mind for more information.*)

SEXUALITY

*'The important thing about acting is to be able to
laugh and cry. If I have to cry, I think of my sex life.
If I have to laugh, I think of my sex life.'*
Glenda Jackson

Sexuality is more than just having sex: it is the embodiment
of all the physical and mental aspects of being a man or a
woman. Sexual intimacy is a splendid thing: it is passion,
it is giving and receiving pleasure, it is communication,
mutual care and regard and at its very best it is deep mental, physical and emotional love between two partners.

An advertising campaign for the Health Education
Council once ran, 'You'd enjoy sex more if you had a pair
of plimsolls.' Think about it.

And finally, you don't have to be young to be sexy.
With age comes confidence, experience, self-awareness,
a deeper relationship, trust, and a more leisurely pace for
love-making.

SHIATSU

Shiatsu, which was developed over 50 years ago by a Japanese named Tokujiro Namikoshi, means 'finger pressure'. The pressure used is much more vigorous than that used in Western-style massage and is usually applied with the ball of the thumb and sometimes even the thumbnail. According to Namikoshi, the pressure should be 'sufficient to cause a sensation midway between pleasure and pain'!

Along with acupuncture, shiatsu shares the concept that there are points on the body (often far removed from the area of pain) which, when stimulated, bring about beneficial results. For example, pressure on the arch of the foot helps aching feet and relieves kidney ailments.

SKIN BRUSHING

A technique for exfoliating, improving circulation and assisting removal of toxins from the body, skin brushing can be done easily before bathing or showering. Use a loofah, dry towel or soft skin brush and brush in circular movements up each arm and leg (your front and back are best done with a towel) always in the direction of the heart. Take care to avoid areas of soft skin such as neck or breast tissue.

'Come, Sleep! O Sleep, the certain knot of peace,
The baiting-place of wit, the balm of woe,
The poor man's wealth, the prisoner's release,
Th'indifferent judge between the high and low.'

Sir Philip Sidney

SLEEP

Our mothers were right about 'beauty sleep' being important, and although there is no definite answer on how many hours is normal, truly restful sleep comes in the first few hours. REM (Rapid Eye Movement) sleep, the dream-time which occurs approximately 90–110 minutes after we drop off, is vital for firing the brain neurones responsible for memory storage and reorganizing information. During the day adrenaline and corticosteroids rush around our bodies, keeping us awake, active and alert. At night during sleep they are replaced by hormones which encourage tissue renewal. If you are lying awake, tossing and turning with your mind whirring, worrying about work and worrying about not being able to get to sleep, adrenaline is reactivated and has an adverse effect on the body. Sleeping pills are not broken down easily by the body and at best are only a short-term solution. Instead, try the following:

❧ Avoid alcohol and caffeine within 3 hours of bedtime and have a warm herbal tea to relax you, such as marjoram, valerian, lemon verbena, passionflower, basil or chamomile.

- 🌿 Leave at least a couple of hours between your evening meal and going to bed.
- 🌿 A banana or small carbohydrate or milky snack 45 minutes before bedtime can help.
- 🌿 Have a warm or neutral (not hot) bath with 2 drops each of juniper and marjoram essential oils.
- 🌿 Massage away neck tension.
- 🌿 Play soothing music or taped sounds such as birdsong.
- 🌿 Do not work in bed, discuss domestic problems late at night or watch television in bed.
- 🌿 Ensure your mattress is firm and your pillow able to give your head and neck good support.
- 🌿 Keep your bedroom dark and cool but make sure you are comfortably warm in bed.
- 🌿 If you still can't sleep, get up and do a peaceful task for a short time and make yourself a nutritious drink. If your head is spinning with worries, write them down on a piece of paper and assure yourself that you will deal with them in the morning.

SMOKING

The health risks associated with smoking are well documented and include: a greatly increased risk of lung cancer, and cancers of the bladder, kidney, pancreas, stomach and uterus; increased risk of miscarriage in pregnant women and increased risk of heart disease and stroke. In addition to these health risks smoking is expensive, antisocial and ageing, it stains your teeth and skin and makes your hair, clothes and breath smell. Smokers have a much lower level of vitamin C in their bodies than non-smokers, leading to lower resistance to disease and accelerated ageing.

The good news is researchers feel that stopping smoking can have an immediate impact on your health. Lung damage can be halted and in some cases reversed, while adverse effects on blood chemistry are quickly counteracted.

There are a number of steps that can be taken to help you give up smoking with the minimum of distress. These include hypnotherapy, aversion therapy, nicotine replacement and acupuncture. However, the most important thing is to want to succeed.

SPOTS

1. Drink lots of water.
2. Eat more vegetables and fruit and fewer refined sugars, refined carbohydrates, saturated fats and dairy products.
3. Include natural oils in your diet, such as those found in nuts, seeds and oily fish.
4. Wash your face with a soap-free facial wash.
5. Don't pick your spots.
6. Use antiseptic cream to help kill the bacteria which cause spots.
7. Pinch and drain toxins from your face by placing the thumbs under your chin, the three middle fingers on top and working outwards towards the earlobes.
8. If your skin condition continues to give you cause for concern, consult a homoeopath, nutritionist, naturopath, doctor, acupuncturist or herbalist. There can be a variety of causes of acne.
9. If drugs are prescribed, check for possible side effects before deciding on that option.

STRESS

'It's not what you eat, but what's eating you.'

Medical proverb

'How beautiful it is to do nothing and then to rest afterwards.'

Spanish proverb

Stress, or pressure, can stimulate us and help us to perform better and achieve more, however, too much stress will take its toll on both the mind and the body in a variety of ways which can lead to mental or physical illness unless we learn to handle the stressors in our lives. A very fundamental and key factor is to be able to recognize that it is not the *thing* that makes us stressed, but our *reaction* to it. Quite often we do not have control over the thing but we always have control over how we react to it, if we so choose.

You can manage stress if you:

☆ Learn to recognize your own optimum stress level: when enough is enough and you need to pull back. Go beyond this and at best the result will be at best decreased performance, at worst, death.

☆ Practise deep breathing and learn yoga, relaxation or meditation techniques (*see pp141 and 106*).

☆ Exercise to 'let off steam', eliminate harmful stress hormones and increase stamina.

☆ Improve diet to include an abundance of vitamins and minerals.

☆ Identify what commonly triggers stress in you and be open-minded and creative about how you can minimize these triggers. Accept that perfection doesn't exist in you or in anyone else: focus on the positive qualities you and others have.

☆ Prioritize and set achievable goals.

☆ Loosen up, smile and don't take yourself too seriously.

☆ A balance of work, play, creative hobbies and quality time with people who are important to you will make you less likely to perceive stress.

SUGAR

Sugar contains no vitamins, protein, fibre or minerals. It is empty calories and, worse, clogs up your system, impairs healthy digestion, is stored as fat and uses up vitamins and minerals. I used to have three teaspoons of sugar in drinks. It took me four months before I could drink a cup of coffee without pulling a face, and now sugary coffee tastes sickly sweet and undrinkable. Good habits take a bit of effort but soon become the natural thing to do. To cut down on your sugar intake:

- Try fruit teas and unsweetened fruit juice.
- Check labels for sugar content.
- Reduce the amount of sugar in recipes you cook for yourself.
- Avoid sugary puddings and replace them with interesting fresh fruit.
- Try sugar-free snack bars and sugar-free jams.

SUNSHINE

We are all aware of the dangers of over-exposure to the sun. But many people do not appreciate the benefits of sunlight. Although we live much of our lives under artificial lights, the more powerful sunlight controls our biological rhythms, stimulating hormones which wake us up and control growth, milk production, egg and sperm production, our metabolism and excretory functions, as well as helping the body assimilate vitamin D.

Lack of natural light and exposure to artificial light for prolonged periods is damaging and energy-depleting. We all know that feeling of zest we get when the first bright spring morning arrives – it's not just the idea that summer is on its way, it is a physical response by the pineal gland to the boost in natural light. Although we can survive without sufficient daylight, our body clocks do eventually get 'out of synch' and can trigger hormone imbalances, sleep and appetite problems and mood disorders. This leads to conditions such as SAD (Seasonal Affective Disorder), which are treated with large doses of artificial light.

THE 10-MINUTE BREAK

No matter how busy you are, take some time for yourself at regular intervals. You will return to your task re-energized and able to achieve more in less time.

- ✤ If you have been sitting, stand and take a full stretch. Do some neck exercises (*see pp88–9*), then shake out each arm and each leg in turn.
- ✤ Walk around for a few minutes, preferably outside.
- ✤ If you have been working on your feet, take the opportunity toit down and put your feet up. Relax, possibly close your eyes and listen to some relaxing or refreshing music.
- ✤ Carry out some slow, deep breathing (*see p23*).
- ✤ Have a healthy snack such as a banana or some raw vegetables such as carrots, celery or mange tout.
- ✤ Have a drink, ideally some water or herbal tea.
- ✤ Maybe phone a friend or family member who has a sunny disposition and focus on positive topics.

TENSION RELEASE

Without realizing it, you tense your body during the day: you clench your jaw, you squeeze your hands on the steering wheel, strain your neck while looking at a VDU, stiffen one shoulder to support a bag or telephone. The exercise below is a lovely one to do at the end of the day to let all this built-up tension flow away:

1. Lie down on your bed.
2. Go down your body clenching and releasing each part in turn: start with your scalp and finish with your toes.
3. As you go, say to yourself, 'I am tensing my arms' (and hold for a few seconds) and then as you release the tension say, 'I am relaxing my arms.'

TUMMY

Many of us have a tendency to put weight on around the waist and tummy, whether as a result of pregnancy, unhealthy diet or sedentary lifestyle.

- Be aware of your posture: stand up straight, holding in your stomach and buttock muscles.
- Do 20 half sit-ups each morning.
- Watch your calorie, fat and sugar intake.
- Regular fast walking, swimming and yoga can all help.

VARICOSE VEINS

Although you can inherit a tendency towards varicose veins, they can also appear during pregnancy and the menopause, if you are overweight, constipated, or if you stand up for long periods.

1 Don't cross your legs.
2 Watch your weight and eat lots of fruit and vegetables to avoid constipation.
3 Eat foods rich in vitamin E, or if appropriate take a supplement.
4 Light exercise such as walking or cycling will help.
5 You may also benefit from taking vitamin C and the plant extract rutin.
6 Put your feet up whenever you can, preferably at a level above your head.
7 Avoid extremes of temperature.
8 Wear support tights.

VISUALIZATION

Mental images are constantly flooding through your brain, and these pictures have a profound effect on your entire system: physically, mentally, emotionally and spiritually, and they have the power to harm or heal you. Visualization is taught by complementary health practitioners as a way of harnessing the power of imagery for good. Phobia sufferers imagine themselves confronting their fears and surviving, cancer sufferers picture their healthy cells overcoming the cancerous cells. Shy people see themselves as happy and confident. Constantly bringing to mind 'as if' pictures will help your body and mind bring the reality about.

VITAMINS AND TRACE ELEMENTS

Vitamin A
Helps protect against infection, maintains mucous membranes, skin and cell membranes.

Sources include: carrots, spinach, watercress, broccoli, watermelon, apricots, eggs and fish-liver oils.

Vitamin B5
Needed for producing antibodies and for adrenal function. Helps with arthritis and allergies.

Sources include: broccoli, peas, cabbage, sesame seeds, cauliflower, whole grains and eggs.

Vitamin B6
A deficiency can cause exhaustion and anaemia. PMS, bloating, morning sickness and stress symptoms may require increased amounts of B6.

Sources include: fish, fresh vegetables, dairy foods, pulses and whole-grain cereals.

Vitamin B12
Required for red cell production and health of the nervous system. Deficiency can lead to fatigue and pernicious anaemia.

Sources include: meat, fish and eggs.

Vitamin C
A deficiency can be caused by alcohol, cigarettes and stress, which in turn can lead to fatigue, a weakened immune system, colds and flu, arthritis and furring of arteries. Step up your intake if you are a smoker, under stress, or if you feel you are coming down with a cold.

Sources include: fresh fruit and vegetables, particularly tomatoes, green peppers, broccoli, citrus fruits, strawberries, blackcurrants and kiwi fruit.

Vitamin D
Vitamin D is needed for hormones and strong, healthy bones, and a deficiency can cause rickets.

Sources: egg yolks, cod-liver oil, mackerel and sardines. It is made by sunlight in the skin.

Vitamin E
Required for effective wound healing, healthy muscles and nerves, and for our cell walls.

Sources include: soya beans, Brussels sprouts, spinach, pecans, walnuts, eggs and whole grains.

Trace elements
We also need small amounts of selenium, iron, zinc, manganese and copper.

Sources include: leafy green vegetables, nuts, seeds, lemons, apples, dried fruits, onions, garlic, tomatoes, asparagus, sunflower seeds, whole grains and honey.

WALKING

Walking is one of the safest, most natural and effective forms of exercise. It can be carried out at any age and by those who are overweight or have health problems which would make other forms of exercise inappropriate. Fast walkers can burn more calories than slow joggers. Benefits include fresh air, daylight and the opportunity to convene with nature. You can use the time for creative thinking or being with a friend or family member. A dog provides excellent motivation and companionship. Invest in the right footwear, start with warm up exercises and pace yourself: begin gently, building up the duration and intensity. Consult your doctor if you have any health concerns.

- Aim for a minimum of 20 minutes fast walking, at least three times a week.
- Walk with a heel to toe action.
- Walk tall, shoulders back, head up, chin parallel to the ground and tummy pulled in.
- Power-walk rather than stroll: you should be slightly puffed, but able to speak and be understood.
- You might like to add on some stretching, toning and breathing exercises.

WATER

We are composed of 75% water and all bodily processes take place in water. Insufficient intake of water can cause anxiety, stress, depression, painful joints, painful periods and constricted blood vessels. Kidneys need to be constantly flushed out, or the toxins gravitate to the liver, which then cannot break down fats effectively.

Make sure you drink 6–8 tall glasses of pure water per day, and avoid drinking during meals as this impairs digestion. If you find it difficult to drink so much water, some of it can be taken mixed with fresh fruit juices or herbal teas.

WRINKLES AND SAGGING

'I always put cleansing cream on in the bath, the steam helps it work. When I finally take it off, my face feels as clean as a chorus girl's conscience.'
Mae West

While growing old gracefully is important, I believe we should make the most of what we have got. The skin's elasticity is maintained by a substance called collagen, a stretchy protein. Oil and water are needed to feed collagen, but over time its elasticity declines, and frown/laughter lines start to appear from the age of around 25. To delay the breakdown in collagen and maintain a youthful appearance for as long as possible:

- ✤ Cleanse, tone and moisturize morning and evening, gently massaging your face.
- ✤ Treat yourself to a professional facial and regularly deep cleanse your face and neck.

- ✿ Take regular aerobic exercise and exercise facial muscles.
- ✿ Moderate your alcohol intake and don't smoke – it is deeply ageing.
- ✿ Lines are worsened by facial tension and furrowed brows.
- ✿ Avoid exposure to harmful elements indoors and outdoors.
- ✿ Increase your intake of fruit, vegetables and water. Nuts and seeds, rich in essential oils, can help avoid premature wrinkles.
- ✿ Vitamin C and rutin can help avoid thread veins.
- ✿ Get quality sleep.
- ✿ Do not sunbathe and wear a wide-brimmed hat and a suitable protection cream when out in the sun.
- ✿ Drink plenty of water throughout the day.

'In the practice of yoga there is a chance to find a gentler strength with which to flow with our lives.'
Paddy O'Brien

YOGA

Yoga is a system of exercises for the mind, body and spirit for which you do not require any great degree of youth or fitness, just a willingness to invest some time and expand your experience. It offers improved muscle and joint flexibility and strength, enhanced heart, lung and digestive function, and eases stress. Some of the postures are recommended for common problems such as back pain, period pain and headaches. Many people also find a sense of inner peace through yoga.

There are many different schools and courses available, and several books and videos. Yoga may be practised by yourself at home but it can be useful to go to a class for the help and inspiration a teacher can give. Meditation and breathing are key aspects of yoga.

CENTRING

TREE POSE

PRAYING STRETCH

COBBLER POSE

'You will do foolish things, but do them with enthusiasm.'

Colette (advice to her daughter)

ZEST FOR LIFE

Try not to get into ruts or routines and rigidity. Instead seek variety – remember it is the spice of life! Allow yourself to be spontaneous, grab the moment and don't become a control freak. Play music that uplifts you, seek the company of people who inspire, amuse and energize you, and be selective about what you read, watch and listen to. Do something 'physical' each day which gets your circulation, joints and muscles moving. Look for opportunities to learn something new each day. Giving to others can be energizing as well as rewarding, but also make sure you give to yourself too: if you keep spending out, without putting something back in, like the bank account, you will dry up and not be much fun to be around. Spend some time with young children, learn to play again and have a good giggle. Actively look for the positive things around you, don't let cynicism creep in and appreciate what you have got, whilst you've got it.

ZINC

A deficiency can cause a weakened immune system, stomach problems, reduced appetite, mental stress, depression and poor wound healing. Zinc is also necessary for collagen synthesis. If you take the contraceptive pill, are feeling stressed, finding it hard to concentrate or are prone to bursting into tears you may need to supplement your diet with extra zinc.

Sources include: eggs, meat, fish, shellfish, whole grains, beans, nuts, seeds, dairy products, ginger and soya.

'Health is the only thing that makes you thnk that now is the very best time of year.'

Franklin Adams

The Sanctuary in Covent Garden is a Day Spa and Fitness Club exclusively for women owned and operated by The Sanctuary Span Group, a company founded originally as Wheway Lifestyle International by Tanya and Allan Wheway in 1989. The Sanctuary Spa Group have recently opened Sanctuary Spas in David Lloyd Clubs located in Sidcup, Stevenage, Chigwell, Milton Keynes, Leeds and Manchester. A Sanctuary Spa and Fitness Club is located in the Lake District within Rank's Oasis Holiday Village and the latest to open is a Sanctuary Health Club and Spa within the new Kensington Hotel, London. All of these Sanctuary Spas welcome men as well as women.

The Sanctuary Spa Group provide worldwide consultancy in the spa business and created and commissioned the award-winning Chiva-Som health resort in Thailand. They are soon to open their first Sanctuary abroad on the Dead Sea in Jordan and have recently launched a range of Sanctuary Spa Products and their first CD.

THE SANCTUARY

Covent Garden, London

A DAY SPA EXCLUSIVELY

FOR WOMEN

Contact:

The Sanctuary
12 Floral Street
Covent Garden
London
WC2E 9DH

Telephone: 0171 420 5151
Fax: 0171 497 0410

for details of day and evening rates and treatments available.